COLLINS AURA GARDEN HANDBOOKS

PRUNING

PETER BLACKBURNE-MAZE

HarperCollins*Publishers*

Products mentioned in this book

'Cutlass'   contains   dikegulac

Products marked thus 'Cutlass' are trade marks of
Imperial Chemical Industries plc
Read the label before you buy: use pesticides safely

Editors Maggie Daykin, Susanne Mitchell
Designer Chris Walker
Picture research Moira McIlroy

First published in 1988 by
Harper Collins Publishers
London

Reprinted 1989, 1991

© Marshall Cavendish Limited 1988

British Library Cataloguing in Publication Data

Blackburne-Maze, Peter
    Pruning. —— (Collins Aura garden handbooks).
    1. Pruning
    I. Title
    635'.0442   SB125

    ISBN 0–00–412391–3

Photoset by Bookworm Typesetting
Printed and bound in Hong Kong by Dai Nippon Printing
Company

Front cover: Pruning *Cornus alba* 'Sibirica'
Back cover: Pruning philadelphus
Both by Ray Duns

CONTENTS

INTRODUCTION

The first question that one usually asks, or is asked, depending on one's knowledge of the subject, is 'Why prune at all?'. It may appear to be simple enough to answer but there is rather more to it than most beginners might imagine.

Some trees can be trained into special shapes by careful pruning. An example of this is the laburnum arch shown here. To achieve this effect, it is essential to start with very young trees.

For a start, a lot depends on what it is that you are pruning. It would be an exaggeration to say that there are as many reasons for pruning as there are things to be pruned, but different groups of plants need pruning for different reasons. Fruit, for example, once it is of sufficient age, is pruned to encourage flower *and* fruit production, whereas a purely decorative shrub is pruned to encourage the production of more flowers. Although these may sound the same, they need a rather different approach, particularly with regard to when the pruning is done.

Reasons for pruning There are, therefore, several basic reasons for pruning; one or more of which can be appropriate to whatever group of plants is being discussed.
• Fruit trees and bushes are pruned so that they produce more flowers, but this has to be extended to encourage fruit production.
• Flowering shrubs, though, are pruned entirely to encourage more and better flowers.
• Decorative-leaved trees and shrubs should be pruned to encourage growth because it is nearly always the young wood that bears

the brightest and best-looking foliage.

• Yet another, but similar, group of trees and shrubs is grown primarily for their decorative stems which are especially attractive in winter. These also need hard pruning to encourage plenty of new shoots.

• All trees and shrubs, however, have to be pruned to keep them both shapely and tidy. This in turn leads to the training of certain plants so that they grow in a definite shape or direction. Cordon fruit trees are an obvious example but, on a rather grander scale, so are avenues of pleached lime trees and laburnum arches (see illustration).

• The clipping of hedges is also a form of pruning. To be of any value, a hedge must be thick, sturdy, impenetrable and not too vigorous. The way that it is pruned or clipped has a lot to do with achieving this.

• There is also a connection between pruning and the health of a tree or shrub. Dead and diseased shoots and branches should always be cut out but this must be done in such a way that the shape and efficiency of the tree or shrub being pruned is maintained.

We can, therefore, fairly neatly summarize the reasons for pruning as maintaining the efficiency, shape and health of the plant in question. Of course, the relevance of these three will chop and change as circumstances and the age of the subject dictate but they will still be there in differing proportions. The art of pruning lies in assessing the relative importance of all these factors correctly and adopting the right method and time for pruning.

Something that must be learnt very early on is the effect that different actions will have on the pruned shoots. Will it encourage growth or flowers? Should a lot or only a little be cut off? All this will be explained later. The difference between the various sorts of bud is shown in the illustration below.

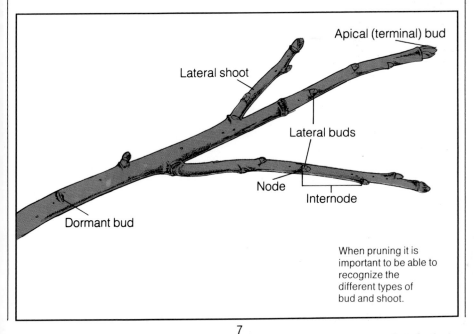

Apical (terminal) bud

Lateral shoot

Lateral buds

Node

Internode

Dormant bud

When pruning it is important to be able to recognize the different types of bud and shoot.

TOOLS AND EQUIPMENT

Like many other jobs in the garden, or anywhere else for that matter, pruning is a skill and, as such, special tools are needed if it is to be carried out properly. Because pruning is concerned with cutting, it follows that everything used must be really sharp. Nothing is worse than blunt tools. They are an abomination – they are neither efficient at their job nor safe for the user.

With this in mind, the various tools which may be used for the various pruning jobs are described below.

Secateurs The standard pruning tool is a good pair of secateurs. These will be used all over the garden, all the year round. When pruning, secateurs are used for cutting through shoots and small branches up to about 2.5cm (1in) across.

There are two basic designs; the scissor and the anvil type. The anvil ones are generally cheaper and operate on the principle of a single blade cutting through the shoot against a hard plastic or soft alloy pad. Provided that the blade is kept sharp and in contact throughout its length with the anvil (by filing down the pad as necessary), they do an excellent job. One criticism is that the anvil is apt to bruise the tissue that it presses against. The importance of this, though, depends on what is being cut. For instance, it will do little harm when pruning shoots on large and mature trees and shrubs whereas it could be a disadvantage when pruning young rose bushes.

The scissor type also has one sharp blade but this passes down the side of a special kind of blade in a scissor action; the contact point therefore has to be kept keen and exact as well. You still get bruising of the lower tissue but, because the secateurs should be used with the cutting blade on the inward side (the tree side), any damage will be on the part that is being pruned off. On the whole, this type of secateur gives a cleaner and neater cut than the anvil sort but a good pair will cost considerably more.

Apart from the actual cutting blade, one of the most important parts of a pair of secateurs is the pivot point. This must be kept oiled and tight enough to prevent any sideways play and wobbling but not so tight that the blades do not operate freely and easily.

Loppers Moving up in the size of branch that is to be cut off, we come to what are usually called loppers. In essence, these are long-handled (about 45cm/18in) secateurs. They are available with either anvil or scissor action. They are intended to be used for cutting out branches too large for secateurs but which are difficult or impossible to reach with a saw. They should not be thought of as a substitute for a saw because the wood may be quite badly bruised and take longer to heal.

They are invaluable for cutting branches out at ground level from shrubs and currant bushes. The long handles make it light work but this is no excuse for failing to keep the cutting blade sharp. Loppers are not an essential tool but they make certain jobs much easier and neater.

Saw There is no doubt that all branches upwards of about 5cm (2in) across should be cut with a saw; the only query relates to the type of saw. For normal work, a small folding saw is perfectly adequate; this will happily cut through branches up to 10–13cm (4–5in) thick.

The larger and more usual pruning saws have either a fixed, curved blade with a pointed end or a straight one with coarse and fine teeth along opposite edges. The latter are also good but you have to be careful that the edge not in use on the double-edged sort doesn't rub against and damage the bark.

Probably the best pruning saws, and certainly the smoothest cutting, are sold under the name of Bridgedale. Instead of being offset, the teeth are straight. The saw is prevented from binding by having the blade hollow ground so that the cutting edge is thicker than the back edge. They are also razor-sharp.

For larger branches, or even for cutting down unwanted trees, a bow saw is a better proposition. You can even go to a chain saw if the job warrants it.

The one thing you must never use is a carpentry saw. The teeth and their setting are all wrong for sawing live, sappy wood and the blade is far too wide and bendy for this sort of work. Besides that, you can easily ruin it if a branch twists and pinches the blade. You wouldn't use a pruning saw for carpentry so why do the opposite? Finally, when using any saw, be careful that it isn't nipped by a twisting branch as this can bend it to the extent of it not returning to its normal shape.

Hedge trimmers For clipping hedges, the choice lies between an ordinary pair of hand shears and electric hedge trimmers. The shears are quite adequate for most average sized garden hedges but, where they are too high or long for comfort, a

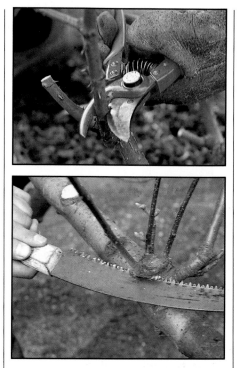

TOP Scissor-type secateurs make cleaner cuts, but are more expensive to buy than the anvil sort.

ABOVE Many pruning saws have a fixed curved blade useful for making cuts at awkward angles.

powered trimmer reduces the time taken to a fraction.

You can now get models powered via cables direct from the mains or running on rechargeable batteries.

Non-essential tools A long-arm pruner is very useful if you have a lot of large trees to prune.

Another non-essential tool is a good pruning knife. Its main use is for pruning young trees as it makes a cleaner cut without the least risk of bruising the bark. It must be as sharp as you can make it. Other tools and gadgets are available but those mentioned are the main ones and are capable of doing anything you are likely to want to tackle.

PRUNING RULES

It is important not only to buy the best tools you can afford but also to know how to use them properly. There are not all that many rules specific to pruning, most are largely a matter of common sense. However, there are some that should always be borne in mind.

A correct pruning cut, made cleanly and close to the bud.

Incorrect pruning cut. The cut is too far above the bud.

The first, and most important, is that you should always have a reason for making each and every cut. Never remove a shoot or branch, or even just a piece of it, simply for the sake of it. If there is no reason for cutting out part of a tree, shrub or bush – don't. When in doubt, leave well alone. You can always take it out later but you can never put it back.

As regards the actual pruning: when using secateurs to cut out a branch that is towards the upper limit of thickness recommended, never force them from side to side to make the cut wider and to prevent binding. All you need to do is bear down gently on the branch and you will cut through it smoothly and easily. If this fails, then clearly it is too thick and you should use a saw.

Again, when using secateurs, always 'cut to a bud'. This means that, when a shoot has been cut, there should always be a bud at the new end; there must never be an inch or so of bare shoot between the topmost bud and the cut end.

Also, the new end bud must be pointing in the direction in which you want the resulting shoot to grow (the one that will grow from the bud in the following year).

The bud is also necessary for the healing over process. If a budless snag an inch long is left, it will usually die and can introduce disease into the shoot. Never leave a snag large enough to hang your hat on, is the age-old rule. Apart from anything else, it looks slovenly.

All saw cuts must be pared smooth and should then be painted, preferably with a proprietary pruning paint. If this is not to hand, then any paint is better than none; the object is to cover the open wound so that disease organisms cannot infect it.

Removing a large branch If large branches are cut off in one piece, their weight will make them impossible to handle. This can be dangerous to the gardener and can make a fearful mess of the tree. The way to prevent this is to cut the branch out as follows.

First, make an upward cut on the underside to extend to about a third of the way through the branch. A cut from above is then made opposite the lower one so that, shortly before the two meet, the branch falls with-

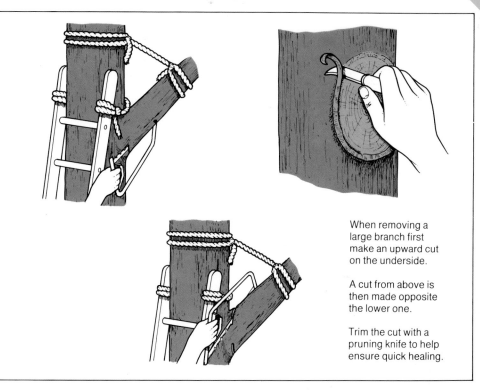

When removing a large branch first make an upward cut on the underside.

A cut from above is then made opposite the lower one.

Trim the cut with a pruning knife to help ensure quick healing.

out tearing a great strip of bark off with it. Watch out, though, it usually parts suddenly and can catch you unawares. Another way of achieving the same end is to cut the branch off about 30cm (1ft) beyond the point where you want it to be finally and then saw off the stump in a separate operation. As always, cut off any branch close to the 'parent' branch, or trunk, for the quickest healing.

Safety first All this talk of 'wounds' and 'healing' reminds one that accidents can happen to gardeners just as much as to anyone else; in the case of pruning, even more so. The reason is obvious: sharp tools are being used.

An interesting point arising from this is that *sharp* tools are far less likely to cut you than are blunt ones. The reason is not at first obvious but it is simply that a sharp tool acts predictably, a blunt one does not. Cutting through a shoot or branch with a sharp knife or secateurs needs very little effort on the part of the gardener; blunt tools need considerable force to make them work and, once force comes into the picture, so do accidents.

You should never be afraid of sharp tools. Use them with conviction and all will be well. If you hold them at arm's length and treat them as though they are about to cut you, in all probability they will. Always make sure that if a sharp tool you are using does slip, neither you nor anything else that matters is in the way. The sort of thing that you have to guard against is having your free hand in the line of fire when using a saw so that, if it slips, the first thing it makes contact with is you.

When trimming a hedge with electric hedge trimmers make sure the cord is running over your shoulder and out of the way of the cutting blades. In case of accidents, it is advisable to have an instant power cut-out fitted to the socket.

Another danger is using secateurs when you cannot see exactly what you are cutting. Ten-to-one your finger will be in the way.

Always, therefore, be in charge of pruning tools. Hold them firmly, use them properly and treat them with respect but, above all, never cut where you cannot see the branch and what you are doing.

Rather different precautions are called for when using electric hedge trimmers – all involved with the cord. This should never be allowed to come between you and the hedge. Have it running over your shoulder and out of the way of the cutting blades. As an added safety precaution, never use electrical tools in wet weather and always have a reliable and instant power cut-out fitted to the power socket in case the cable does by chance get cut.

The effect of pruning We saw earlier why pruning is desirable, now we should look at how a woody plant responds to pruning. As a rule, it is very simple because pruning encourages growth. If a one-year-old shoot is cut back, it sends out two, three or even four new shoots from buds near the cut end. This is a useful function when shaping young trees or rejuvenating old ones.

However, pruning should never be overdone on flowering shrubs or fruit trees and bushes which are of bearing age because it can induce a lot of new growth at the expense of flowers and fruit. This is often the price that has to be paid for reducing the size of a tree or shrub or when you actually want to encourage the production of new growth.

Cutting back larger branches also increases the vigour of those nearby, especially the one to which the branch has been cut back.

On the other hand, pruning certain fruits in the summer encourages the development of fruit buds and at the same time reduces extension growth (see page 40).

WHEN TO PRUNE

This section deals with the more practical aspects of pruning; what to do and, even more important, when to do it. However, you should first understand that, if a tree, shrub or bush is never pruned at all, very little harm, if any, will come to it, but it will grow less well. At the worst, a flowering shrub will become straggly, top heavy and will produce fewer and smaller flowers. Much the same will happen to a fruit tree; it will become congested, it will produce fewer and poorer fruits and there is likely to be an increase in pests and diseases.

From this it can be seen why pruning is beneficial to most woody plants, if not a matter of life and death. There is just one more principle that we should look at before discussing the subject more specifically and this concerns the timing.

The time of year at which pruning is done will influence the performance of plants more than anything else. The flowering season of flowering trees, shrubs and climbers is an excellent guideline as to when they should be pruned as this indicates whether the best and most flowers are being produced on the current season's or last year's growth. An example of each will make it clear.

The popular shrub forsythia flowers in the spring and, therefore, produces the best of its flowers on shoots that grew during the previous season. Older shoots also flower, of course, but not in such profusion.

Bush roses (hybrid tea and floribunda), on the other hand, send up new shoots which flower in the same season as that in which they grow.

The forsythia flowers in spring and produces the best of its flowers on shoots that grew in the previous season. Some are also produced on older shoots, but they are not such good quality.

LEFT *Spiraea* × *bumalda* 'Gold Flame', a summer-flowering shrub, is cut back quite severely in spring.

BELOW Forsythia is pruned immediately after flowering, removing old flowered shoots.

Therefore, in general, ornamental trees and shrubs which flower before about mid-June are doing so mainly on the shoots that grew last year. Those that flower later than that are doing so mainly on the current season's shoots. A plant should be pruned so that the right-aged shoots predominate and, broadly speaking, the way to do this is to apply one very simple rule, which is, in fact, the key to the pruning of most ornamental trees and shrubs.

• Those that flower in the first half of the year mainly on shoots that grew last year (e.g. forsythia) should be pruned immediately after flowering is finished.

• Those that flower from about July onwards, should be pruned in the late winter or early spring.

Obviously there are exceptions, but this rule can normally be relied on to work and is very easy to follow. It does, though, only apply to ornamental trees, shrubs and woody climbing and wall plants.

Following this rule allows the maximum amount of time to elapse between pruning and the next flowering period, and ensures the longest growing time and the production of the greatest number and size of new shoots.

Evergreens The main exceptions are most evergreens and conifers. They should normally be pruned in April, regardless of their actual flowering time.

Fruit Fruit trees and bushes are rather a special case and are pruned at a convenient time after the crops have been gathered; usually in the winter. This has the added advantage of being the time when they are leafless and it is, therefore, easier to see what to prune.

It isn't always as simple as this, though, because many fruits benefit from another and different kind of pruning during the summer to improve the quality of the fruit and to encourage the formation of fruit buds for the following year. This is covered fully in the fruit section (page 38) but, briefly, the situation is that apples and pears are pruned during the winter with some types of tree, e.g. cordons, also receiving treatment in July/August.

Stone fruits (plums, cherries, peaches, nectarines, apricots, etc.) are pruned in the late winter or early spring just before they start into growth with, again, some being pruned and trained in summer during the growing period.

Currants and gooseberries are normally pruned in early autumn during leaf-fall but red and white currants and gooseberries also benefit from summer pruning.

Cane fruits, such as summer-fruiting raspberries, blackberries, loganberries, tayberries, sunberries, tummelberries and other hybrids, should be pruned straight after fruiting. Autumn-fruiting raspberries are best left until March.

In many cases, the summer pruning of fruit trees, bushes and canes is coupled with tying them in to wires and training them.

Hedges These are also something of a special case and are described in more detail on page 34. In general, though, they are best clipped twice a year, in May and August.

Privet may need three or even four clips and flowering hedges, such as *Berberis* × *stenophylla*, are usually best dealt with at the same time as they would be if they were being grown as specimen shrubs.

A hedge of the evergreen *Berberis* × *stenophylla* is best pruned immediately after flowering, but do not cut it too hard or there will be fewer blooms produced the following year.

TREES AND SHRUBS

When pruning trees and shrubs, there is a clear distinction between pruning for growth and pruning for flowers; this takes us back to two of the reasons for pruning – 'formation' and 'maintenance'. In the early years of a woody plant's life, we must be concerned solely with shaping it and encouraging it to grow well and into the right shape. If the plant gets off to a good start and grows in the right direction, its future as an attractive and useful garden plant is assured.

Remember also that shoots and even buds are much easier to remove from a young tree than are branches from an older one; a lot of 'pruning', therefore, will be directed to the removal of buds or juvenile shoots that have only just started to form.

Training a tree When dealing with a young tree, whether ornamental or fruit, the important thing is to start it off properly. It must have a clearly defined trunk of the desired height and any shoots or branches growing from below that point must be removed (see illustration below).

Pay particular attention to the formation of the main branches. If these are already formed when you buy the tree, ensure that they are growing where you want them to. If they are not, prune them back and start again.

If they are where they should be, probably all that will be needed is to cut back by about a third of their length any new shoots that you wish to form more side branches. When doing this, always cut to a bud pointing in the direction in which you want the new main shoot to grow. As a rule this will be away

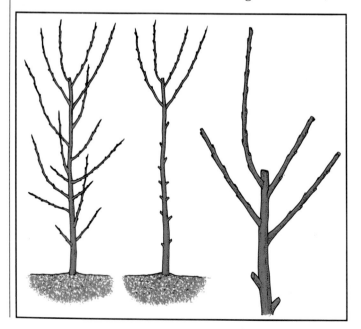

A young standard tree must be properly pruned from the beginning, removing any shoots from the trunk that are not needed and shortening any that are required as side branches. At least four strong shoots will be needed to form the head of branches.

16

from the centre of the tree but this is not always so. Sometimes you may wish to direct the new shoot towards filling a gap.

Pruning mature trees Once the tree reaches flowering age (this will vary enormously with the species), pruning should be aimed at encouraging flowering, which will really mean that less pruning is required – heavy pruning encourages growth at the expense of flowering. Ornamental trees need very little attention after the first ten years or so. Once the framework of branches has formed and they get into a flowering pattern, they tend to look after themselves. Maintaining the shape is all that is normally required when pruning.

Pruning shrubs Most flowering shrubs, on the other hand, need a constant supply of young shoots to keep them looking their best. This is achieved by removing either parts of branches or complete branches (down to ground level) once it looks as though they are past their prime and the quality of flowering is deteriorating. As a rule this normally takes about five years.

Obviously, out-of-place branches should be dealt with as necessary to maintain the shrub in a good shape. This will involve either their partial or complete removal as soon as trouble is spotted.

Conifers Many conifers, both trees and shrubs, are grown on a single stem and not as a stool. A stool is a shrub that has many shoots growing at or from below ground level, such as our old friend forsythia.

To maintain the shape of conifers, little pruning is needed beyond the removal, as soon as they are seen, of any out-of-place shoots or of double leaders. If two leaders are formed, you should retain the more upright and remove the other back to the main stem.

Ground-covering conifers of the juniper type must be encouraged to branch out from an early age by pruning back any shoots that seem to be growing more strongly than the rest. Rigidly shaped conifers, such as *Juniperus virginiana* 'Skyrocket', should have any wayward shoots tied back into the body of the tree rather than cutting them out. This latter course usually creates a nasty and unsightly bare gap.

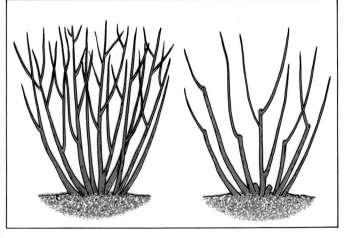

Most flowering shrubs need a constant supply of young shoots and this means regularly cutting out some of the old wood, which is deteriorating in vigour. Here typical shrub pruning is shown, before (far left) and after.

17

WHAT AND WHEN TO PRUNE

This is a list of some of the more popular shrubs with details of how and when they should be pruned, along with any idiosyncrasies they might have. Occasionally, trees and shrubs may need very hard pruning either to rejuvenate them or to restore their shape. Not everything will stand this harsh treatment, mention is made of those that will not.

AUCUBA If needed, prune hard in April. Otherwise, lightly for shape in the summer.

AZALEA Little needed beyond shaping. Cut back long shoots after flowering is finished.

BERBERIS The deciduous types should be pruned, if necessary, in February; the evergreens in April or after flowering. When *B*. × *stenophylla* is grown as a hedge, prune back long shoots after flowering; do not clip or the informality is destroyed.

BUDDLEIA The shoots of *B. davidii* varieties that have flowered are pruned hard back in February or early March. Other species after flowering is finished.

CALLUNA (Ling heather) Clip back with shears in March to tidy up and encourage bushiness.

ABOVE The shoots of *Buddleia davidii* varieties, like 'Harlequin', are pruned hard back in early spring.

LEFT Cytisus or broom should only be pruned lightly, after flowering, as cutting into old wood can result in die-back. The attractive and rather unusual hedge illustrated is formed from two varieties of cytisus.

BELOW *Cornus alba,* and its varieties like 'Sibirica', must be cut back hard in March (left) to encourage a crop of new stems which have the most brightly coloured bark.

CAMELLIA Very little needed. Cut back straggly shoots after flowering to improve the shape.

CARPINUS (Hornbeam) See Hedges.

CARYOPTERIS Cut back the previous year's flowering shoots fairly hard in March to encourage new growth.

CEANOTHUS Prune spring-flowering evergreens after flowering. Late summer/autumn-flowering varieties are pruned in early spring to encourage new flowering shoots to form.

CHAENOMELES (Quince) Thin out crowded branches and shorten back side shoots, if necessary, in late April/early May after flowering.

CORNUS (Dogwood) The shoots of those grown for their coloured stems are cut hard back when new growth starts in the spring.

COTINUS (Smoke bush) No regular pruning when grown as a bush but may also be grown as a stool when the previous year's shoots are cut back to two buds every spring.

COTONEASTER Deciduous kinds in February; evergreens in April. All respond well to hard pruning when they get leggy and outgrow their position in the garden.

CUPRESSUS Pruning is restricted to maintaining the trees as a single stem and removing out-of-place, damaged or dead shoots and branches. Do this in April.

CYTISUS (Broom) Prune lightly after flowering to prevent legginess, to maintain shape and to encourage new flowering shoots. Never prune back into old wood as broom seldom sends out new shoots from this.

DAPHNE Should never be pruned unless essential and then only after flowering (March).

DEUTZIA Prune in summer after flowering to maintain shape and to encourage new growth. Remove older shoots and branches once the quality of the flowers deteriorates.

ELAEAGNUS Prune evergreen species in April; deciduous in February. Prune only for shape but old bushes may be cut hard back into old wood for rejuvenation.

ERICA (Heath) Clip with shears after flowering to maintain bushiness. Replace with new plants every ten years or so.

ESCALLONIA Remove worn-out wood from early-flowering varieties after flowering. Leave those that flower in autumn until the following spring. Prune to maintain shape.

FORSYTHIA After flowering, prune the flowered shoots back fairly hard to maintain the supply of new shoots; these flower the best.

FUCHSIA Treat more or less like herbaceous plants and cut down to the ground in March. In very mild districts, this harsh treatment is unnecessary as the shoots will not survive the winter.

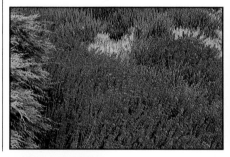

ABOVE After flowering, clip ericas or heaths lightly with shears to remove the dead flowers and maintain a bushy habit of growth.

LEFT Hebes should be pruned only in spring and can if necessary be pruned back hard to maintain shape and compactness. Young growth is quickly produced from the old stems.

LEFT Keep hydrangeas young by removing old and weak shoots and branches once growth starts in the spring (below). Also remove dead flower heads at this time.

GAULTHERIA Old shoots are best removed after flowering to retain shape and vigour.

GENISTA (Broom) Treat the same as Cytisus. Do not cut into old wood.

HAMAMELIS (Witch hazel) Prune only for shape and to keep open. Attend to this in April or during the winter when the prunings may be brought indoors to flower.

HEBE Any pruning should be carried out in spring. Cut back leggy bushes to maintain shape and compactness. May be cut back very hard after frost damage as soon as new growths have started to appear.

HELIANTHEMUM (Rock rose) Prune or clip back straggly shoots after flowering to keep the plants bushy.

HIPPOPHAE (Sea buckthorn) Tolerates the very hard pruning sometimes necessary to stop the bushes getting leggy. Do this in February/March. Otherwise, prune only for shape, also in spring.

HYDRANGEA Keep the bushes young by removing old shoots and branches once growth starts in the spring. Also, leave dead flower heads until spring to protect the buds. The climbing *H. petiolaris* needs little pruning beyond shortening back in spring shoots which have grown too far out from the wall or fence.

HYPERICUM In March prune lightly for shape and to encourage new flowering shoots. *H. calycinum* should be clipped in the spring to within a few inches of the ground every two or three years.

Holly or ilex, including variegated varieties, may be cut back hard in April to maintain shape. Hollies also make good hedges, which need regular trimming.

ILEX (Holly) May be cut hard back in April to maintain shape. See also Hedges, page 34.

KERRIA (Batchelor's buttons) For best results, prune to the ground, or nearly so, after flowering. Pull up any unwanted suckers.

LAVENDER Clip back in March/April (better than after flowering) to retain compactness and tidyness Avoid cutting back into old wood.

LIGUSTRUM (Privet) See Hedges.

LONICERA See Hedges for *L. nitida* See also Climbers. The winter flowering *L.* × *purpusii* and other shrubby honeysuckles require no regular pruning other than for shape or to encourage the production of new flowering shoots.

MAGNOLIA Very little pruning is normally required, any should be carried out in late July. Keep the shrubby types growing and shapely by careful removal of old, damaged or out-of-place branches.

MAHONIA *M. japonica* should be encouraged, when young, to branch. Little further pruning needed.

PAEONIA (Tree paeony) Cut out dead flower heads in winter and dead shoots in summer. Occasionally remove old and worn-out branches.

PHILADELPHUS (Mock orange) After flowering, remove completely all old branches that are no longer producing flowering laterals. Also, any branches that are out-of-place. Overcrowding and old branches quickly cause deterioration.

PIPTANTHUS Prune in spring or early summer once any winter damage has been assessed. Cut back dead and overcrowded shoots and branches either to the ground or to new and younger ones.

POTENTILLA Prune in the spring by cutting out weak and short growths to make room for stronger. These, if excessively long, should be cut back by half to encourage the production of flowering side shoots.

PRUNUS Beyond shaping in their early years, flowering cherries and coloured-leaved plums do not require pruning. Laurel hedges should be pruned with secateurs as necessary each spring or early summer.

PYRACANTHA The best specimens are trained against a wall, often as fans. Once the framework has been formed, side shoots not required are cut hard back after flowering.

RHODODENDRON More important than pruning is the provision of the correct growing conditions, especially that of acid soil. Any pruning for shape or the removal of dead shoots or branches should be carried out immediately after flowering or in April. The latter if severe treatment is needed.

RIBES (Flowering currant) All wood older than about five years should be cut out completely to keep the bushes young and full of flowers. Normally, though, remove old and worn-out branches after flowering. Any very hard pruning should be done in winter.

ROSEMARY Cut back any straggly or winter-killed shoots and branches in April. Encourage young plants to bush out by removing shoot tips.

TOP *Philadelphus coronarius* 'Aureus' can be pruned after flowering. Cut back old branches.

CENTRE AND ABOVE Prune philadelphus by removing all old flowered growth.

SALIX Willows grown as trees need little pruning after the initial branch formation. Those grown as stools for the beauty of their winter bark should be cut hard back in March, or every other March. Treat the dwarfer pussy willows similarly but prune after the catkins have finished flowering.

SKIMMIA Pruning is seldom needed except to retain shape and compactness. Prune in spring if necessary.

SPIRAEA Prune spring-flowering species, such as *S.* × *arguta* and *S.* × *vanhouttei,* after flowering by removing old, worn-out and out-of-place shoots. Summer- and autumn-flowering, e.g. *S. japonica* and *S.* × *bumalda* 'Anthony Waterer', should be cut back hard in February to encourage many new flowering shoots to form.

SYMPHORICARPOS (Snowberry) Pruning not needed except to remove dead shoots. Best grown where its suckers cannot spread invasively. Pull up, don't cut, any that are surplus to requirement.

LEFT Willows grown for their coloured bark, like *Salix alba* 'Vitellina', are cut back hard in March to a framework of old wood *(above)*.

LEFT Prune weigela after flowering by removing the oldest branches and any that are spoiling the shape of the bush.

BELOW Usually lilacs require only light pruning and the removal of dead flower heads, and this is best done immediately after flowering. Straggly bushes can be cut back to half their height in winter but this means a loss of flowers for a time.

SYRINGA (Lilac) Any hard pruning to restore shape, etc., should be done in the winter. Light pruning and the removal of dead flower heads is done immediately after flowering. Avoid damaging the new, soft shoots when carrying this out.

TAMARIX (Tamarisk) *T. tetrandra* flowers in May/June and should have the flowered shoots shortened after flowering. *T. pentandra* flowers in late summer/autumn and should be pruned back almost to the main branches in February.

VIBURNUM If flowering well, little pruning is needed. If deciduous shrubs are getting old or top-heavy, cut out some of the oldest branches in winter, regardless of their time of flowering. Lighter pruning for shape is best left until after flowering. Evergreens (e.g. *V. tinus*) may be pruned hard in April to restore shape, if need be.

VINCA (Periwinkle) *V. major* may be cut back with shears to within 10–13cm (4–5in) of the ground in spring every two to three years if necessary and to keep it in bounds. *V. minor* may also be cut then but it seldom needs it.

WEIGELA Prune after flowering in June/July by removing the oldest branches and any that are spoiling the shape of the bush or causing overcrowding of the branches.

PRUNING ROSES

Some types of rose require a lot of pruning, others very little. On the whole, the hybrid tea and floribunda types need most attention and the species roses the least. These last may be either shrub or climbers.

A weeping standard rose is an ideal choice of tree for a small garden. The variety 'Excelsa' is illustrated. When pruning, cut back the shoots that have flowered and retain the new growth for flowering the following year.

Hybrid tea After winter planting, the bushes should be cut down to within 7.5–10cm (3–4 in) of the ground. This will encourage quick establishment and the production of strong shoots in the following year. Thereafter, the bushes should be tidied up and headed back by shortening all the main branches in November.

'Proper' pruning is carried out in March when any weak shoots are completely removed. Those remaining are shortened back to not more than 30cm (1ft) long. Some gardeners prune far harder than this but it reduces the number of flowers in the following summer and makes them later; they are, though, bigger.

Remove all dead flowers. This is called 'dead-heading'.

Floribunda These are pruned in exactly the same way as hybrid teas but, because they are grown for their massed colour effect and not for perfect single blooms, pruning is less severe. Leave the shoots 60cm (2ft) long after March pruning. Dead-head as before.

Climbers These are pruned in two ways and with two aims in view. In their early years, they must be encouraged to grow and fill the space allocated to them. After that, they should be pruned so that there is a balance between flower production and growth.

After winter planting, cut them down as you would a new floribunda. During the formative years, the shoots must be tied in as they grow.

Most of the new shoots will be long and strong. These may be shortened to encourage branching if desired, but not by more than about half.

Once they start flowering, it will be seen that the flowers develop on side shoots (laterals) growing on the main branches. These laterals are cut back to 2.5–5cm (1–2in) long in the spring.

Once a main branch produces only second rate flowers it should be removed. Dead-head whenever it is necessary during the summer.

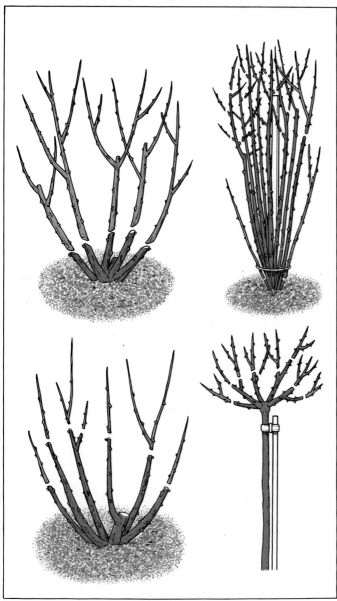

TOP FAR LEFT
Hybrid tea roses are pruned in March, by removing all weak shoots, after which all strong shoots are cut back to within 30cm (12in).

TOP LEFT Climbing roses are pruned by having side shoots (or laterals) shortened in the spring.

BOTTOM FAR LEFT Floribundas are pruned in the same way as hybrid teas but not as severely.

BOTTOM LEFT Standard roses have their heads pruned as for bush roses but all the shoots should be of the same length.

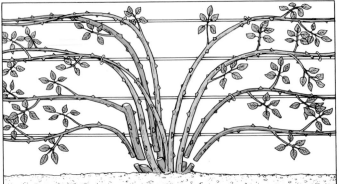

Rambler roses are pruned after flowering by cutting down to the ground all the old flowered shoots.

Shrub and species roses Most of these are treated as flowering shrubs. They need little attention beyond keeping them in good shape and removing worn-out branches in the late winter.

On no account dead-head them until you are familiar with them as many produce attractive hips in the autumn and this is one of their main attractions.

Most climbing species, e.g. *Rosa banksiae*, are the best when pruned only for shape.

Ramblers Although, at first sight, similar in appearance to climbers, ramblers send up new shoots from the ground each growing season. These will simply grow in the first year; it is not until their second year that they flower. During growth they should be tied in loosely to prevent being damaged.

They will produce an explosion of flowers in the following summer. After that, the flowered shoots are cut down to the ground and the new ones are tied in to flower next year.

ABOVE LEFT Ramblers bloom freely in summer.

ABOVE Species roses do not need much pruning.

CLIMBING PLANTS

Although it is usual to think of climbers, and other plants that can be induced to climb, in terms of clothing walls and fences, you must never forget that they also provide some of the finest ways of covering up unsightly sheds, garages, etc. Another very attractive use for climbers is to grow them up into trees which, for one reason or another, are not particularly good looking in themselves.

Climbing roses are really unnatural climbers as they have to be trained and tied in to some type of suitable support.

The distinction between a climber and a wall shrub is not always easily seen but the broad classification is that there are self-clinging climbers (ivy, clematis, etc.) and climbers that need help in the way of supports and ties, such as winter jasmine and climbing roses. Then there are plants that are not really climbers at all but which are trained and tied to a wall or fence, e.g. pyracantha and ceanothus. To this last group can be added many tender plants that need the extra warmth of a wall to help them survive. They do not need it for climbing up or for clinging to, merely for protection.

Quite clearly there is no standard way of pruning climbers because there is as great a diversity amongst them as there is in any plant group. Available space is a major factor.

Natural climbers Some of these need little or no attention at all;

they include such things as Virginia creeper and ivy which are equipped with clinging pads and aerial roots respectively, that fasten onto whatever it is they are climbing up or over. You may have to encourage them to cling to the surface in the first instance but, once anchored, they will romp away on their own.

The best way of getting them to hang on is to push a split cane into the ground by the plant so that the top end is firmly against the wall. Tie the plant to the cane and all should be well.

Climbers that hold onto things with tendrils (vines) or by twining round them (honeysuckle and wisteria) can also be left largely unpruned but they usually flower much better when given proper attention. Where space is not limitless and especially with certain clematis (see later), it will be necessary to keep them restricted.

LEFT The honeysuckle is a natural climber as it twines around supports. It needs little pruning.

BELOW Clematis are also natural climbers and where space is restricted some will need reasonably hard pruning.

A natural climber that often presents problems is wisteria. Not so much because it won't grow or climb but because it is often reluctant to flower. Like it or not, it must be said that there is great variation in the strains of wisteria available; some flower well and early, others seem never to. The problem is that you only find out which strain you have after a number of years.

Unnatural climbers This covers plants that are certainly climbers but which need quite a bit of help from us to make them climb. Ramblers is probably a better word for them. Winter jasmine is a good example. It should always be trained and tied to a trellis or something; never left to fend for itself or it will end up like a jungle.

There are no real pruning rules for this group. As with all climbers, they should first be trained to cover the area intended for them but, after that, they can be pruned to their individual requirements.

Non-climbers These are plants that we tend to train against some kind of surface although they don't need it for support. The main reason for this treatment is that the wall or

fence against which they are grown offers them protection against the temperature and/or the weather and this is really the sole object of this method of growing.

The system is used almost exclusively for plants of doubtful hardiness like ceanothus, camellia, fremontodendron (fremontia) and, often, escallonia. If they are the sort that can be trained to fill a given area, then this should be done first. Once it has been accomplished, the shrubs are pruned in the same way as they normally would be.

Most of these will already have been dealt with in the Trees and Shrubs section starting on page 18, others will appear below.

POPULAR CLIMBERS AND WALL SHRUBS

CLEMATIS These have always had a sort of aura surrounding them so that their treatment has been shrouded in mystery. There is absolutely nothing mysterious about them at all, as more or less the same rules and techniques apply that have already been discussed.

The spring- and early summer-flowering species, such as Cs. *montana, alpina* and *macropetala*, can perfectly well be left untouched if there is enough room for them. Much the same goes for the later (May/June) flowering C. *patens* and *florida* varieties. If any of these do need pruning, it should be done by cutting them fairly hard back straight after flowering.

The Lanuginosa group that flowers from June to October can either be left alone or pruned hard back in February. Leave them alone if they are flowering well and have not outgrown their position.

The Jackmanii and Viticella groups need rather harsher treatment. They flower on new shoots throughout the summer and autumn and should be cut hard back every February. This not only keeps them neater and more compact but also produces the best blooms. To this group can be added the later-flowering species such as C. *tangutica* and C. *flammula*.

To summarize it all: late-flowering varieties may be pruned hard in February but those that flower in the spring and early summer may be left, if space permits. If not, prune after flowering.

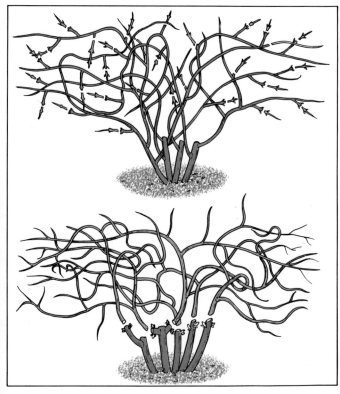

TOP Spring and early summer flowering clematis may need nothing more than judicious thinning out.

BOTTOM Late-flowering clematis may be pruned hard in February, almost down to the ground.

COTONEASTER The species most normally grown against a wall is, paradoxically, *C. horizontalis*. Provided that it is planted no more than about 15cm (6in) from a wall, it will use it as a support by itself. The only pruning needed will be for shape.

HEDERA (Ivy) No real pruning is required but variegated varieties should be attended to regularly to remove any shoots that have reverted to a non-variegated form. After a hard winter, many ivies will have suffered damage, these should be clipped hard back against the wall to remove dead and damaged foliage and shoots and to encourage new growth to take its place.

HYDRANGEA PETIOLARIS See Trees and Shrubs, page 21.

JASMINE (especially *J. nudiflorum*, winter jasmine) Winter jasmine is first built up as a framework of shoots to cover whatever you are training the plant against. Once this is done, pruning for flowers can start. This must be carried out every spring after flowering. Of the shoots that grew in the previous year, the weak ones are cut out completely, the remainder are cut hard back to 2.5–5cm (1–2in). It is from these that next year's flowering shoots will grow during the summer. Any strong shoots that are required for filling up spaces are left long and are tied in to the supporting framework. Thin out any overcrowded growth.

Summer jasmine, *S. officinale*, is a vigorous climber and is usually left alone and allowed to scramble at will over its support.

Wisteria is pruned by cutting back all new shoots in July (top), and further reducing them when the plant is dormant in winter.

Allow wisterias to cover allotted space, or 3 to 4 years to elapse, before you start regular pruning, which encourages the development of flowering spurs.

LONICERA (Honeysuckle) This should first be trained over the area intended for it. Once that is done, the plant should be kept young by the occasional removal of the older growths. These are replaced by tying in younger shoots.

After flowering, the laterals that bore the flowers may be cut back to their basal buds to encourage these to grow out and form flowering laterals for the following year. Summer-flowering varieties may be pruned after flowering; evergreens, and those flowering later in the year, in March/April.

PASSIFLORA (Passion flower) The aim is first to create a semi-permanent framework of vines from which flowering shoots are then encouraged to grow. After the formation of the framework against the support, the young shoots that flowered in the previous year are cut back to the basal buds in the spring. There is often some winter mortality of the shoots and this treatment will encourage strong new growth.

POLYGONUM BALDSCHUANICUM (Mile-a-minute, Russian vine) Aptly named and not to be planted where it needs to be restricted. It climbs by twining so only needs to be pointed in the right direction at planting time. No pruning is needed beyond the occasional clearing out of dead material from the centre once it is well established.

WISTERIA Forming the framework of vines is easy enough, you simply tie them to wires or a frame so that they cover whatever it is that you are training them to. The problem lies in reducing their vigour and getting them to flower.

Once the plant has covered the allotted space, or when you have been training it for 3 to 4 years, a spur system should be built up on the main vines as it is these spurs that will produce the best flowers. Spurs are formed by cutting back all new and unwanted shoots to 15cm (6in) in July and, further, to two buds in December/January. That is all there is to pruning wisteria.

HEDGES

As with all pruning, it has to be said again that very little harm will result from cutting a hedge at the 'wrong' time; at worst it may suffer some damage during the winter from the cold killing immature shoots. Unlike pruning, though, not cutting a hedge is certainly bad practice and there are definitely 'right' times for doing it.

RIGHT Yew, when grown as a formal hedge, is best trimmed in late summer, ideally using shears.

LEFT The golden-brown winter leaves of a beech hedge. This subject is trimmed in late summer or early autumn.

Hedges are grown for different purposes, but this should have been taken into account when planting them. The main reasons for having one are for privacy, to keep out people and animals, to provide shelter from the weather, to hide an unpleasant view or to form a protective screen against noise. These will all have a bearing on the choice of plant used but it is important, if the hedge is to be effective, to look after it properly.

Hedges fall into three different categories: formal, semi-formal or informal. Semi-formal is not always easy to identify.

Formal hedges Those which are kept trimmed to rigid lines. They are usually grown from slow-growing evergreens and conifers such as box, holly and yew.

Box and holly are best clipped in July or August and yew a month later. If any drastic cutting back into old wood is needed, May is the best time of year to do it.

Semi-formal hedges Most of us, though, are content with the lower standard of semi-formal hedges which are quicker growing but not of such a high quality. They are represented by plants such as privet, *Lonicera nitida*, hawthorn and conifers that are clipped just once or twice a year, according to the standard required and the growth made.

These form the vast majority of hedges and are best clipped either in May or in May and August. Incidentally, serious thought should be

given before planting privet or lonicera; both can be more trouble than they are worth as a hedge and there are many better to choose from. In fact, they should be clipped as often as they need it during the growing season to keep them in bounds and looking tidy.

Beech, on the other hand, is a first-rate hedging plant but should be left untrimmed for its first two growing seasons to allow it to establish itself and to start growing. After that, clip it in late summer or early autumn. This treatment will lead to the dead leaves being retained during the winter.

Laurel hedges are quite popular in some districts but it would be wrong to be in too much of a hurry to plant one. They are not reliably hardy and may suffer damage in a hard winter. This usually takes the form of browning of the leaves. Added to that, they have to be pruned with secateurs, not clipped with shears. If the leaves are cut by clipping, not only do they look terrible with the cut edges going brown, but careful pruning with a pair of secateurs has to be done to put matters right.

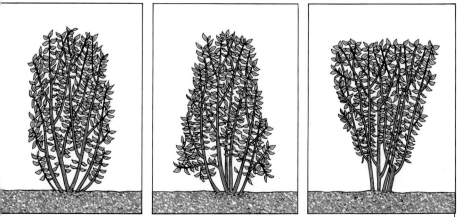

The ideal hedge should be clipped so that it is wider at the base than at the top (as at left and centre). The rather top-heavy hedge shape (right) is not recommended.

Chamaecyparis lawsoniana, the Lawson cypress, makes an excellent formal hedge, even quite tall if desired, which can be trimmed in spring.

Informal hedges These are a very different matter and are normally grown more as a visual barrier or a windbreak than as a physical one to keep people and animals out. However, this latter attribute can be achieved if plants with prickles are grown, such as berberis and roses.

Cultivated blackberries trained along wires make perhaps the best prickly hedge of all; they are rather like fruitful barbed-wire. The pruning of this only involves the removal of the oldest canes to keep the hedge fruiting and effective.

The important thing with the decorative informal hedges is to tie down the vigorous young shoots for the first few years so that no growth is wasted and a barrier is soon formed. After that, the hedge is treated in roughly the same way that an individual shrub of the same sort would be. If it is a rose hedge, it would be tidied up in November and pruned properly in March. Naturally, though, it would be kept much taller than one would a single bush.

Berberis × stenophylla is a particularly good informal hedge, the long willowy shoots are shortened back as required after flowering.

There are several *Cotoneaster* species that also make good hedges.

These are treated in much the same way as the berberis.

Clipping An important aspect of cutting any hedge is the shape that it should be. A hedge must always be broader at the base than at the top. This keeps the base thick and prevents the whole thing becoming top-heavy and blowing over in high winds or being broken apart by snow. This shaping should start from the hedge's first clipping.

Saving labour Many people regard the clipping of hedges as an irksome task that they can well do without. The ultimate in labour-saving devices must surely be the use of the hedge growth retardant 'Cutlass'. When applied to most kinds of hedge after an initial cutting in the spring, no further attention is needed during that growing season.

For those who like a certain amount of work, but not too much, one of the several electric hedge trimmers makes light work of the job. The range available includes a cordless model with a re-chargeable battery.

Where only a small amount of work exists, a good pair of shears and secateurs will do admirably.

POPULAR HEDGING PLANTS

Type	Shape	Recommended Height	When and how to cut
Beech	Formal	1.5m (5ft)+	Clip in August or May & August
Berberis stenophylla	Informal	1.8m (6ft)	Prune after flowering
Box	Formal	Up to 90cm (3ft)	Clip in July/August
Holly	Formal	1.5m (5ft)+	Clip or prune in July/August
Hornbeam	Semi-formal	1.5m (5ft)+	Clip in August or May & August
Laurel	Formal or semi-formal	1.5m (5ft)+	Prune in spring
Lawson's cypress	Informal	3–4.5m (10–15ft)	Prune or clip in spring
Leylandii	Informal	4.5m (10ft)+	Prune or clip in spring
Lonicera nitida	Formal or semi-formal	Up to 1.2m (4ft)	Clip as required
Privet	Informal	1.2m (4ft)+	Clip as required
Yew	Formal	1.2m (4ft)+	Prune or clip in August/September

PRUNING FRUIT

To many people pruning fruit is as mysterious a task as pruning roses but, as with roses, there is nothing complicated once you master a few basic principles. Fruit trees come in many shapes and sizes but the two that are by far the most popular and easily managed in gardens are the bush tree and the cordon-trained tree.

The renewal system of pruning, which is designed to replace old branches, is highly recommended for standard pear trees as it keeps them young and fruitful.

The bush is a free-standing tree in the open ground; the cordon is trained against wires and/or canes which may be against a wall or fence or, again, in the open ground. Most kinds of tree fruit can be grown in one or both of these two forms and the bonus is that the different ways of pruning them can be adapted to many other tree forms as well.

Thus we find that standard and half-standard trees are pruned in the same way as bush trees whilst the system for cordons is appropriate for espaliers as well. There are, of course, differences in pruning the various kinds of fruit but even this is simpler than you might think because several kinds can be grouped together under the same banner.

APPLES AND PEARS
These are pruned in the same way and are grown in the same tree forms. The two most common methods for pruning bush apple and pear trees are the 'regulated' system and the 'renewal' system.

Regulated system This is the simpler and involves the removal of only those branches and shoots which, for one reason or another, need to go. The reason could be any one or more of the following: overcrowding, dead, diseased or broken branches, one shading another, those that are too high, too low or crossing from one side of the tree to the other. In fact, any branch or shoot which is not carrying out its job or which is preventing others from doing theirs.

While this method of pruning is easy to carry out and improves the appearance and general well-being of the tree, it is only of limited benefit with regard to improving the crop in terms of quality and quantity of the fruit produced.

Renewal system This method is designed to do all that the regulated one does, and in addition keeps the tree young and, therefore, cropping well and heavily. The previous guidelines still apply but they should be carried out with the emphasis on one particular aspect: to make sure that the tree is furnished with plenty of *young* wood.

To achieve this, if a branch is too high, too low or just too long, it should be cut back to a younger one nearer its point of origin. Similarly, if two branches are competing for space, preference is normally given to retaining the younger. In this way, every main branch will have younger replacement branches being built up on them to take over when the leader is removed.

Very few shoots are tipped as this can delay fruiting; tipping is restricted to shoots on those branches which are being built up to replace older branches. As such, its aim is to induce the development of side shoots and, hence, the fruiting complexes or 'spurs'.

Both these systems are perfectly easy to follow and carry out if you bear in mind what they are designed to do. The regulated system is a sort of annual winter service; the renewal system is designed more to 'renew' old branches and those that are past their best or become diseased.

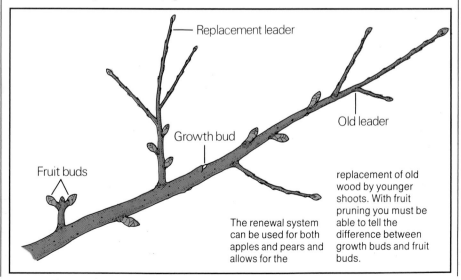

Replacement leader

Old leader

Growth bud

Fruit buds

The renewal system can be used for both apples and pears and allows for the replacement of old wood by younger shoots. With fruit pruning you must be able to tell the difference between growth buds and fruit buds.

39

Early training Bush trees will usually start cropping when they are 4 to 5 years old and, in the years preceding this, the emphasis must be on laying down the framework of the tree. Shoots that are wanted for branches are cut back by a third in the winter to a bud pointing in the required direction. The aim should be to build up a head of 8 to 12 young branches; most other growths can then be treated as fruiting laterals.

Cordons and espaliers These terms refer to two 'intensive' ways of growing apples and pears, which occupy far less space while producing good crops.

Cordons are single-stemmed trees furnished with fruiting spurs but with no branches. They are planted at a 45 degree angle to encourage

TOP Cordon-trained apples (and pears) are highly recommended for small gardens as they take up minimal space but produce good crops of fruit.

LEFT Cordons are pruned mainly in late July and early August when all side shoots are cut back to one or two buds.

fruiting and to discourage vigorous, unwanted growth.

The main pruning is done in late July and early August when all side shoots are cut back. Those arising directly from the main stem are cut back to two buds (about 5cm/2in long). Those growing from already shortened shoots (spurs) are cut back to one bud (2.5cm/1in). In the winter, any soft growth formed after summer pruning is cut out.

Espaliers are a form of extended cordon and consist of a central vertical stem and pairs of horizontal branches trained out from it at regular intervals. Pruning is exactly the same as for cordons except that it takes longer to form the complete tree and, obviously, shoots required to form branches should be cut back in the winter and then only by half.

TOP Apples can also be fan-trained if desired and should be summer pruned in a similar way to cordon-trained apples.

LEFT Pears (and apples) can also be grown as espaliers against a wall. In this instance pruning is the same as for cordon-trained fruits.

PLUMS AND CHERRIES

Plums are grown almost entirely as bush trees; cordons are seldom a success due to the excessive vigour of plum trees. It is also possible to grow them fan-trained against a wall if a sufficiently large area is available.

Plums should be pruned as little as possible and only in the very late winter or early spring. This is to prevent infection by the silver leaf fungus which enters wounds during the winter. Pruning along the same lines as the regulated system (described on page 39) is the most successful.

Cherries should be treated the same but remember that, unless grafted on a dwarfing rootstock such as Colt or Inmil, they take up much more room than the majority of small gardens can spare.

Other stone fruits (peaches, nectarines and apricots) are really only successful when fan-trained against a warm south- or west-facing wall. Fan-trained trees are pruned according to the principles given under cordons and espaliers.

TOP The Morello cherry is invariably trained as a fan against a wall or fence. This is a young tree – eventually it will take up quite a bit of wall space.

LEFT A Morello cherry in fruit. When trained against a wall it is much easier to protect the fruits from the ravages of birds.

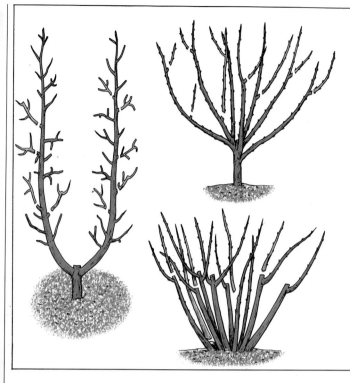

FAR LEFT Cordon gooseberries grown as a U-shape against a wall or fence. Cut back new shoots to four or five leaves in summer and prune again in winter.

LEFT ABOVE Red currants can also be grown as bushes and in winter all new shoots are cut back to form a spur system.

LEFT BELOW Blackcurrants are grown as bushes which are encouraged to produce plenty of young growth by cutting back older branches.

GOOSEBERRIES AND RED CURRANTS.

These are pruned in the same way and both may be grown as either bushes or 'U' cordons trained to a wall or fence.

The bushes are grown on a short trunk (leg) and should be made up of semi-permanent branches; these being cut out to make room for younger ones only when the quality and quantity of their fruit begins to deteriorate.

During the formative years, cut back by a third the shoots intended to form branches each winter (much the same as for bush trees). Once the bush has formed, all new shoots that appear are cut back to two buds in the winter so that a fruiting spur system is created on the branches.

Alternatively, summer pruning can be carried out in late June when new shoots are cut back to about five leaves. This is followed by the previously mentioned winter pruning.

Summer pruning encourages quicker ripening and bigger fruits.

BLACK CURRANTS.

Never prune these like red currants because they produce their best fruit on shoots younger than about four years old. As such, they must be encouraged to grow as well as fruit by applying fertilizer each spring.

Pruning consists mainly in cutting out to the ground branches that are four and more years old to make room for younger ones. Along with these, you should remove branches that are too low, or otherwise clearly out of place, and those which are causing overcrowding. Diseased and broken branches must, of course, also be removed.

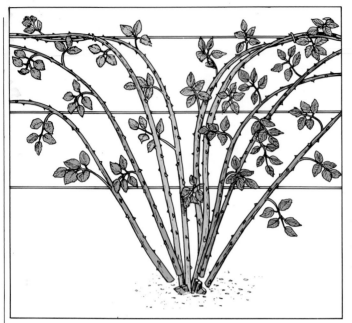

Blackberries and similar cane fruits are pruned immediately after fruiting by cutting down to the ground all the old stems or canes that have borne fruits. The young canes are tied in to the supporting wires.

CANE FRUITS

This covers raspberries, blackberries, and the hybrid berries – loganberries, tayberries, sunberries and the new tummelberry.

They all grow and fruit in the same way. The shoots (canes) grow during one year and fruit during the next. Pruning is very simple: the canes that have borne fruit are cut down to the ground straight after fruiting. After this, the new canes are tied in to the supporting wires.

In the case of summer-fruiting raspberries, the canes should be spaced approximately 10cm (4in) apart along the top wire.

The exception to this pruning-after-fruiting routine is autumn-fruiting raspberries, the fruited canes of which are left standing until the following March.

The layout of supporting wires for raspberries and those for the other cane fruits differ. For summer raspberries, the wires should be stretched between strong supporting posts at intervals of 60cm and 1.5m (2 and 5ft) above the ground, whereas for the other and more vigorous kinds, they should be 90cm, 1.2 and 1.5m (3, 4 and 5ft). Another at 1.8m (6ft) is helpful for tying the new canes to during the summer.

Autumn raspberries don't need a post and wire system but should have taut twine run down each side of the rows to stop the growing canes falling over.

The other cane fruits are dealt with rather differently. In fact, any one of several systems can be employed. The easiest is the 'two-way rope' system. With this, the new canes are trained upwards and then outwards along the 90cm, 1.2 and 1.5m (3, 4 and 5ft) wires on each side of the plant; the 1.8m (6ft) wire being kept for the next lot of new canes. This method has the advantage of keeping the fruiting canes and growing canes apart, making them healthier and easier to manage and control.

AXILLARY BUD The bud at the base of a leaf.

BASAL BUD One of the cluster of buds produced at the base of a one-year-old shoot.

CLIMBER A plant which has the ability to climb either on its own or with the help of the gardener.

DECIDUOUS (adjective) A tree or shrub which loses its leaves each autumn and grows more in spring.

EVERGREEN A tree or shrub which retains its leaves all year round.

FLOWER BUD A bud which will develop into a flower and then, if appropriate, into one or more fruits.

FRUIT BUD see Flower bud.

GROWTH BUD A bud which will grow out into a new shoot.

LATERAL (Side-shoot) A shoot which develops on an older stem or branch other than at its tip.

Spur systems in flower.

LEADER The shoot which develops from the tip of an existing shoot or branch. May also refer to the end section of a branch.

LEGGY Referring to a shrub, or tree, lacking in side-shoots with all its growth and leaves towards the top.

LONG-ARM PRUNER A device for pruning shoots and small branches well beyond one's normal reach.

SHOOT A stem that is one year old or less in age.

SNAG The short length of shoot wrongly left beyond the topmost bud when a shoot has been cut back.

SOFT FRUIT Fruits which grow as bushes or canes; e.g. currants, gooseberries, raspberries etc., also strawberries.

SPUR That which remains when a shoot is cut back to 2.5–5cm (1–2in) long. (See page 39.)

STONE FRUIT Plums, cherries, peaches, etc. Fruits which have a stone in the centre.

STOOL Method of growing a shrub in which most new shoots come from below ground; e.g. some salix and cornus, also black currants.

TERMINAL BUD The bud at the tip of an unpruned shoot.

TIPPING The removal of the top few inches of a shoot to induce side shoots to form.

TOP FRUIT Tree fruits; e.g. apples, pears, plums, cherries, etc.

THE YEAR'S WORK

March is a good time to prune climbing roses.

Below are some of the main events in the pruning year. Full details of dealing with all the different subjects mentioned will be found in the main body of the book.

JANUARY/FEBRUARY

Prune deciduous trees and shrubs and fruit trees except during very cold weather.
Leave those flowering in winter and spring until flowering is over.
Prune late summer- and autumn-flowering clematis.

MARCH

Finish pruning deciduous subjects and late summer clematis before growth starts.
Prune plums, damsons and cherries.
Cut down any autumn-fruiting raspberry canes.
Prune all roses except ramblers.
Prune hard back cornus and salix stools grown for their winter stems.

APRIL

Prune decorative trees and shrubs that have finished flowering.
Prune evergreens and conifers.
Clip or prune evergreen and conifer hedges, apply 'Cutlass'.

MAY

Prune trees and shrubs that have finished flowering.
Start summer pruning peaches.
Clip deciduous hedges. Apply a growth regulator such as 'Cutlass'.

JUNE

Summer prune gooseberries and red currants.
Prune back to sound wood any shrub that was badly damaged by frost during the winter.

JULY

Prune and tie in rambler roses.
Start summer pruning apple and pear cordons, espaliers, fans, etc.

AUGUST
Continue summer pruning apples and pears grown as cordons, fans, espaliers or other trained forms.
Carry on pruning and tying in rambler roses after flowering.
Cut down raspberry canes once they finish fruiting and tie in new canes.
Clip deciduous hedges.

SEPTEMBER
Prune hybrid cane fruits after fruiting and any remaining summer-fruiting raspberries.

OCTOBER
Continue pruning and tying in hybrid cane fruits and blackberries after fruiting.

NOVEMBER
Start pruning deciduous trees and shrubs, also fruit trees and bushes as soon as the leaves have fallen. Lightly prune and tidy up climbing, hybrid tea and floribunda roses.

DECEMBER
Continue pruning deciduous trees and shrubs and fruit.

Prune buddleia in March.

Conifer hedges can be pruned in April.

INDEX AND ACKNOWLEDGEMENTS

Picture credits

Pat Brindley: 13,15,18(t),20(t,b), 21,22,23(b),25(t), 28(l,r),30(t),33,36,38,40,41(t),42(t,b),45.
Harry Smith Horticultural Photographic Collection: 4/5, 9(t,b),12,23(t),25(b),30(b),35,41(b).
Michael Warren: 1,6,14(t,b),18(b),19,24,26,29,34.

Artwork by Simon Roulstone